Hop, Skim, and Fly

An Insect Book by
ROSS E. HUTCHINS

Parents' Magazine Press • New York

CONTENTS

A grasshopper. Note that its body is divided into three parts. The feelers or antennae, the eyes, and the mouth parts are on the head. The middle section, or thorax, has three pairs of legs and two pairs of wings. The back part of the body is called the abdomen.

CHAPTER 1

THE INSECT WORLD

The small animals we call insects are found almost everywhere. You can see them in fields, woods, ponds, and city parks—even in your home. There are nearly a million different kinds of insects. Most of them neither harm us nor help us. But some eat our crops, destroy our houses, or spoil our food. Other insects are useful. Honeybees make honey and wax. Shellac comes from lac insects. Many insects are useful because they eat the ones that are harmful to us.

But, harmful or useful, almost all insects are interesting to study and watch. In this book you will meet some of the more common and interesting kinds, especially those you are most apt to see.

Some insects, such as butterflies, are very beautiful. Others—cockroaches for example—are not pretty at all.

All insects have an *outside* skeleton, *three* pairs of jointed legs, usually *two* pairs of wings, and *three* body divisions.

A grasshopper is a typical insect. Look at one very carefully and you will see that its body is divided into three parts. The front part is the *head,* and just behind this is the *thorax*—the middle, or chest section. The back part of the body is called the *abdomen.* On the head you will see the feelers or *antennae,* the eyes, and the mouth-parts. There are *three* pairs of legs and *two* pairs of wings. The legs and wings are attached to the middle section or thorax.

Most insects, such as grasshoppers, bees, and butterflies have two pairs of wings. Flies have only one pair. Some insects, such as lice and silverfish, have no wings at all.

THE LIFE STORIES OF INSECTS

Most insects hatch from eggs. At once they begin to eat and to grow larger. When the young insect's tough skin, or shell, becomes too tight, a split opens down its back and the insect crawls out of its old skin. The new skin is a little larger than the old one. As the insect continues to grow, its skin is shed, or *molted,* several times. After each molt the insect is a little larger than it was before. It is like a boy getting a new suit of clothes each time his old ones become too tight. That is the way a caterpillar grows.

After a caterpillar has molted several times it is full grown. It is now ready for the next step in its life story. If it is a butterfly caterpillar, it hangs itself up by its tail, usually under a leaf or twig. Then it sheds its skin again. That changes it into the resting or *pupal* stage. It is now called a *chrysalis.* A chrysalis cannot eat or move about.

This butterfly caterpillar is in the chrysalis stage. It has hung itself on a window screen, which is very unusual.

After several weeks the chrysalis splits open. An adult butterfly crawls out. At first its wings are damp and crumpled up. Soon they become larger and dry out. Then they are stiff, and the butterfly is ready to fly.

A moth caterpillar spins a silken cocoon around itself before it changes into the resting or pupal stage. After several weeks the adult moth crawls out of the cocoon. Then it, too, is ready to fly.

So we see that butterflies and moths have *four* steps in their life stories. These are: egg, caterpillar, pupa, and adult. This is called a *complete* life story.

EGG   ADULT

COMPLETE METAMORPHOSIS

CATERPILLAR (LARVA)   CHRYSALIS (PUPA)

This black swallowtail butterfly has four stages in its life history: egg, larva (caterpillar), pupa (or chrysalis), and adult. This is a complete life history, or metamorphosis.

7

Grasshoppers grow in a different way. When they come out of the egg, they look like grasshoppers, but they are very tiny. They shed their skins as they grow larger, and each time they look a little more like adult grasshoppers. Such young 'hoppers are called *nymphs*. After the last molt they become full-grown grasshoppers. Then they mate and lay eggs.

Grasshoppers' life stories have only *three* steps: egg, nymph, and adult. This is called a *gradual* life story. Many other insects besides grasshoppers have gradual life stories. These include aphids, stink bugs, praying mantises, and cockroaches.

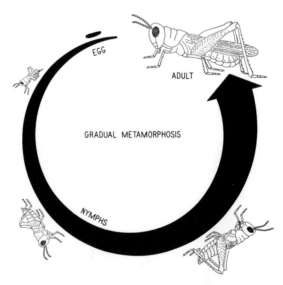

EGG

ADULT

GRADUAL METAMORPHOSIS

NYMPHS

Grasshoppers grow up in three stages: egg, nymph, and adult. This is known as a gradual life history or metamorphosis.

CHAPTER 2

INSECTS OF HOMES AND GARDENS

A number of insects live in our houses. Most of these
are pests and we try our best to get rid of them.

COCKROACHES

Cockroaches are the worst household pests. Some are
very tiny. Some, like the American roach, are more
than two inches long. Some roaches have wings and often
fly. Others have no wings at all.

Usually these insects hide in cracks in woodwork or
behind shelves during the day. At night they come out of
hiding and rush about looking for food. Cockroaches
have rather dirty habits. They may carry germs to the
uncovered foods they eat. Their eggs are enclosed in little
brown capsules. They drop these capsules on shelves or
in drawers. Later, the young roaches hatch out.

Cockroaches are among the oldest insects. For millions
of years they have lived in forests, and most kinds still
do. Only a few kinds come in to our homes. Wild

A cockroach

cockroaches can often be found under the bark of dead trees or in decaying logs.

SILVERFISH

Another insect often seen in our homes is the silverfish. Usually they are found on shelves behind books or among old magazines. They eat book bindings or other starchy materials. Silverfish are less than half an inch long. They have three slender tails. These insects prefer darkness. They hide in cracks during the day. When they are frightened, they dart away like tiny fish. Their bodies are covered with fine silvery scales. That is why they are called silverfish.

Cockroach eggs are enclosed in small brown capsules.

A firebrat is a
kind of silverfish.

One kind of silverfish insect is the firebrat. It is
known by this name because it often lives near a fireplace
or in some other warm place. Most kinds of silverfish
insects are found among dead leaves or under the bark of
fallen trees.

HOUSE FLIES

House fly young, or *larvae,* are called maggots. They
live and feed where there are rotting plants or animals.
Often the places they live in are very dirty. When the
maggots change into adult flies they may carry germs to

A house fly

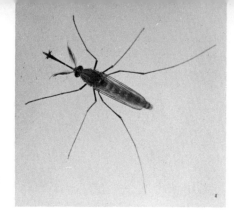

A mosquito

foods they light on. House flies are about a quarter of
an inch long. They have only one pair of wings.

There are many other kinds of flies. Fruit flies lay their
eggs on fruit and their maggots feed inside the fruit.
The maggots of screw-worm flies live in the wounds of
cattle and other animals. Horseflies are blood-sucking
insects that annoy horses and other livestock.

MOSQUITOES

Like house flies, mosquitoes are common almost
everywhere. They suck blood through their needle-like
mouth-parts and so often make us miserable outdoors
in summer. Their larvae, or wigglers, live in water. They

Mosquito larvae, or wigglers, live in water.

A mud-dauber wasp with its clay nest.

are often found in old cans or buckets. For this reason such containers should always be turned bottom-side up.

Mosquitoes of some kinds carry serious human diseases. These include malaria and yellow fever. These diseases once caused sickness and many deaths in the United States. They still do in many very hot countries.

MUD-DAUBER WASPS

Often, on the walls or ceilings of porches, we see the clay nests of mud-dauber wasps. These wasps gather clay from the edges of pools or other damp places. They carry the clay to the places where they are building nests. If you break one of these nests open you will see several cells. Usually these cells are filled with spiders that are only half alive, because they have been stung by the wasp. The young, grub-like wasps eat these spiders.

There are two different kinds of mud-daubers. One kind—the black and yellow mud-dauber—builds its cells side by side. The other kind—the organ-pipe wasp— builds its cells end to end in long rows. That is the reason

13

it is called the organ-pipe wasp. It is interesting to watch the wasps carrying their loads of clay and using them to build their cells.

GARDEN INSECTS

Many insects live in flower and vegetable gardens, and often damage the plants. Plant lice, or aphids, are common garden pests. They are tiny, green insects that gather on the stems or leaves and suck the sap. Sometimes they kill the plants they live on. Aphids can often be seen on rose stems, but you have to look closely because they are almost the same color as the stems.

Aphids are sometimes called "ants' cows" because ants protect them from enemies. In return, the aphids make a sweet material called honeydew which the ants like very much. If you watch an aphid colony for a while you may see the ants "milking" their "cows." You may also see a ladybird beetle eating the aphids. When this happens the ants become very excited and drive the little beetle away from their "cows."

Ladybird beetles are pretty insects. Usually they are red with black spots, or the other way round. They are the aphids' worst enemies and are always looking for them. When you see ladybird beetles hurrying about over leaves, you may be sure that they are looking for colonies of aphids. Their young also feed on aphids.

Wherever there are gardens there are insect pests. There are cutworms that hide during the day and come out at night to eat the flowers and vegetables. Cutworms

Ladybird beetle eating aphids on a plant.

A stink bug

turn into the "millers" or moths that fly to lights at night.
There are also leaf-eating beetles that destroy the leaves,
and stink bugs that pierce the stems and leaves to get
their sap. Stink bugs are less than half an inch long and
have flattened bodies. When you touch them they give
off a bad smell.

You can sometimes see little masses of bubbles or foam
on the stems of garden plants. If you look closely you
will see small insects hiding inside each foamy mass.
These are spittle insects. They make the little masses of
foam and live inside them. The foam protects them
from enemies. They feed by sucking out the juices of the
plants they live on.

Many insect pests eat corn. Sometimes, when the green

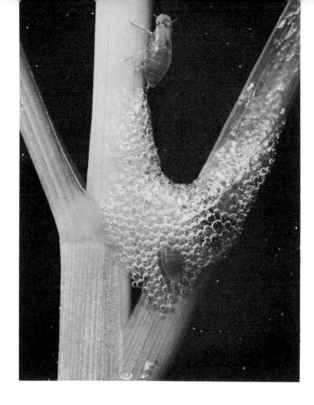

Two spittle insects on a plant with the mass of bubbles they make to live in.

shucks are taken off the ears of corn, plump caterpillars or "worms" will be found inside. These are corn earworms. When they are full-grown the corn earworms change into millers. The leaves of corn are often eaten by grasshoppers. Grasshoppers also eat other kinds of plants.

Several insects cause damage to tomatoes. Large caterpillars called hornworms eat the leaves. They are called hornworms because each one has a small horn on its tail. They are about three inches long. The adults are hawk moths.

Garden plants of several kinds are often damaged by mealybugs. These are plump, white insects without wings that suck out the sap. Sometimes they kill the plants.

17

CHAPTER 3

SOME INSECTS LIVE IN COLONIES

Insects that live together in colonies are called social insects. They are probably the most interesting of all insects.

THE BEES

Honeybees are useful insects that live in busy, city-like colonies. More than 80,000 honeybees may live in one colony. In a way, a hive or colony of bees is a family. They are all related to each other. There is one queen, and thousands of workers. The workers are females but they cannot mate and lay eggs. They do all the work of the colony. The queen is much larger than the workers. Her only duty is to lay eggs. The other bees in the colony are all her children, including the drones. Drones are the male bees. They are smaller than the queen.

When one home gets too crowded a queen and several hundred workers fly away. This is called a "swarm." They gather together in the form of a ball, which usually hangs from a tree limb.

Here is a queen bee on the comb with workers all around her. The workers feed and clean her.

To find a new home, scout workers fly away in different directions, each one looking for a place that will do. After a time, these scouts come back. They "tell" the rest of the bees about the places they have found. They do this with special bee dances. This is the way bees communicate, or give messages to each other. Some of the scouts have, perhaps, found hollow trees. Others may have found spaces between the walls of houses. As the scouts go on dancing, the swarm "decides" which place they want. Then they all fly away to their new home.

If they have chosen a hollow tree, they at once begin to clean it out and get it ready for building wax comb. Bees are very clean creatures and their new home must be made spic and span.

At left: Honeybees are
usually kept in wooden hives,
but they sometimes live in
hollow trees like this one.
During the day, the worker
bees fly out of the knot-hole
to gather nectar and pollen
from the flowers.
Below: Honeybee workers on
their wax comb. In each
hive there may be as many as
80,000 bees.

This honeybee is on the flower of a pear tree. It carries the pollen in clusters on its hind legs.

The wax-maker bees quietly cling to the inside walls of the hollow tree. Slowly, tiny scales of wax form under their abdomens. The bees remove these wax scales and shape them into six-sided cells.

In the meantime, other bees have been gathering nectar from flowers in the nearby fields. The nectar is placed in the new cells and is slowly changed into honey. Then the openings of the cells are sealed with wax. Other bees gather pollen from flowers and this is stored in other cells. All the bees are busy, except the drones, or males. The queen has been busy, too. In some of the cells she has laid eggs, one egg in each cell. When the eggs hatch, the bees will be workers. After the eggs hatch the young bees, or larvae, are fed and cared for by adult workers. Their food is a mixture of pollen and honey.

21

When the larval bees have finished growing they are sealed in their cells. Then they change into pupae. After a week they begin to break out of their cells. Now they are adult worker bees. At first, they work inside the hive. They clean it out and care for the young bees. Later, they will join the field bees to gather nectar and pollen. Some of them will become scouts who fly away to the fields to find new patches of flowers. This is important work.

When a scout finds a field of flowers, it returns to the colony and begins its "honey dance." The dance "tells" the other bees where the flowers are. The scouts also "tell" the field bees what kind of flowers to look for by giving them samples of the nectar they have found. Soon, the field bees fly away and begin to gather the nectar.

As the weeks pass, there are more and more worker bees and so the colony in the hollow tree grows larger and larger. More wax combs are built, and they are stocked with honey and pollen. By autumn the colony is ready for cold weather. Honeybees keep warm by forming themselves into a tight ball, or cluster. Now and then during the cold months they eat some of their store of honey. When spring comes at last, they again begin to gather pollen and nectar and raise young bees.

When a hive becomes too crowded the workers build some special wax cells. The queen lays an egg in each of these cells. The cells are larger than the ones for worker eggs. They hang downward with their openings at the bottom. The eggs are glued to the bottoms of the cells

This queen honeybee has just come out of her cell.

and so do not fall out. When the eggs in these special cells hatch, the young bees are given special food. It is made by the worker bees and is called royal jelly. Bees that are fed royal jelly grow up to become queens.

As soon as the first new queen comes out of her wax cell she gnaws into all the other queen cells and kills them. Soon after this she flies out of the hive and mates with a drone. She then returns to the hive. When the old queen leaves the hive, she takes several hundred workers with her. And that is how a new swarm begins.

Bumblebees have habits very much like those of

Bumblebees are much larger than honeybees and have very fuzzy bodies. They are black with white or yellow markings. This one is sucking nectar from a zinnia.

honeybees. These large, fuzzy bees build their nests in the ground. Usually they prefer old mouse nests. Like honeybees they gather pollen and nectar from flowers as food for their young. In autumn all the bumblebees die except the mated queens. These queens spend the winter under logs or other protected places. In spring they start new colonies.

THE ANTS

All ants live together in colonies and their lives are, in many ways, like those of honeybees. There are hundreds of different kinds of ants. Some of their colonies are very tiny, with only a dozen or so in each one. Other kinds of ants live together in very large colonies. Sometimes more than a million ants live in one colony.

Most ants are not harmful, but a few kinds are pests in homes and some harm crops.

Many kinds of ants, such as the tropical army ants, live by hunting insects and other "game." They stream through the jungle capturing various small creatures. These ants have no real homes. They usually stay in stumps or under logs long enough to raise their young. Then they move on again.

Leaf-cutting ants live in warm countries. These ants cut small sections out of leaves and carry them into their underground nests. A special kind of food is grown on the leaf sections. The leaf-cutting ants live in the southern part of the United States, and in Central and South America.

A colony of black and red carpenter ants with their white young, or larvae.

Many ants build their nests under the earth or under stones. Others tunnel through wood or live in the hollows of twigs or plant stems. Carpenter ants gnaw passages through solid or partly rotted wood. Their food is mostly insects that they capture near their homes. These large ants live in most places in the world.

Trap-door ants live in trees. They are very interesting. These ants make their tunnels inside the twigs of white ash and other trees. Some trap-door ants in each colony have plug-shaped heads. These ants use their heads like stoppers to close the entrances to their tunnels. This keeps enemies out.

Scattered about over our western prairies are cone-shaped ant mounds. Each one is surrounded by a bare, sandy space. A harvester ant colony lives in each of these mounds. They eat seeds that they gather from plants. There are several thousand ants in each harvester ant colony. Each one has a queen, many wingless workers, and a number of soldiers. The soldiers protect the colony. In the spring there are a few males in each colony. The males have wings.

Each morning in summer the workers leave the nest. They hurry away through the grasses and other plants that grow near the nest. These ants are searching for seeds. The seeds they find are carried back to the nest. They are put in special "grain bins." Later, other workers take the husks off the seeds and carry them to the outer edge of the bare, sandy space.

The worker ants use their file-like tongues to file the husks off the starchy seeds. The seeds are food for all

A cone-shaped mound on the western prairies built by harvester ants.

Harvester ants live under the mound in "nests" or chambers like these. There are seeds in some chambers and young white ants in others.

the ants — the workers, the queen, and the young ants.

The ants are always busy. Some workers gather seed. Other workers dig new passages and nests in the ground. Often, some of these tunnels go down as much as five feet. These deep nests are below the frost-line and the ants spend a cozy winter in them.

These interesting ants often gather and store a quart or more of seed. But sometimes their seeds are stolen. Prairie gophers and kangaroo rats often dig into the nests and eat the seeds the ants have so carefuly gathered.

In spring, new queens and males, with wings, fly out of the underground nests and mate. After mating the males die, but each queen flies away and digs a small tunnel in the ground. She then bites off her wings. Once she has mated, she does not need her wings any more. She then lays a few eggs. When these hatch, she cares for the young ants herself. There are no workers in the

A large paper nest built by bald-faced hornets. The nests hang from the limbs of trees. The entrance hole is near the bottom.

tunnel to help her. Later, when the young ants are grown up, they are workers. After this the queen has help and never again leaves the nest. Soon the colony gets bigger. After several years have passed there are many, many workers, all busy at the tasks in the nest. This is the way a new ant colony begins.

THE PAPER HORNETS

Many of us have seen the large nests of paper hornets in the woods. Some are more than a foot across. These are the homes of bald-faced hornets. If it was summer and we were wise we left them strictly alone. Hornets sting badly, so winter is the best time to look into such a nest. By that time, the nest is empty. All the hot-tempered hornets have been killed by the cold.

If you cut open one of these nests you will see that the

A bald-faced hornet at the entrance to the nest.

A bald-faced hornet collecting wood fiber from a dead tree to build a nest.

outer walls are made of several layers of paper. This paper is made of plant fibers that the hornets have gathered from dead trees and fence posts. Inside the paper nests are several rows of cells, also made of paper. These cells are six-sided and look something like the ones honeybees build out of wax.

The hornet colony lives in this well-built nest all summer. The worker hornets are hunters. They capture caterpillars and other insects and feed them to their grub-like young in the cells. Like queen honeybees and queen ants, the queen's only duty is to lay eggs.

Just before the cold weather some males and new queens hatch out. The males die after mating, but the queens find sheltered places, usually under the bark of dead trees, and settle down for the winter. They do not move again until the spring sun warms the woods.

In the spring, each young queen starts a new hornet colony, usually under a tree limb in the woods. Like the harvester ant queen she must, at first, do all the work herself. She gathers fibers and builds a round nest about the size of a golf ball. Inside this she makes several paper cells and lays an egg in each one. When the eggs hatch she has to work very hard because she must hunt food to feed the growing young. After the first hornets come out of their cells the queen no longer has to work so hard. She has their help. As more and more hornets come out of the cells, the nest is made larger. But all the hornets, except the queens, will die before another winter comes.

When the cold weather comes, queen yellowjackets find safe places to keep warm. This one is under a rotten log.

The queens live to continue the chain of hornet life from one summer to the next.

There are a number of other kinds of hornets. Yellowjackets build paper nests in cavities or holes in the ground. Other hornets, known as *Polistes* wasps, build clusters of paper cells attached to plants or to porch ceilings. These cells are not enclosed in paper walls.

THE TERMITE CLAN

To most people termites—often called "white ants"—are pests that destroy houses. But they have most interesting lives. They are social insects of a special kind.

The termites are closely related to the cockroaches.

31

They are white, soft-bodied insects that tunnel through wood. The wood also provides their food.

There are several thousand termites in a colony—workers, soldiers, kings, and one queen. The workers are blind. Kings and queens start life with wings but later shed them.

Some workers and soldiers are male and some are female. None of them has wings. The soldiers have large jaws. They defend the colony. Like other social insects, the queen termite's duty is to lay eggs. Old termite queens may become quite large, with their abdomens, or bellies, swollen with eggs. The queens of some termites that live in hot countries are often two or three inches long. In a termite colony the large queen does not always lay all the eggs. Other termites, known as *supplementary* queens, also lay eggs.

At certain seasons, especially in spring, young kings and queens swarm out of the nest and pair off. These pairs stay together while looking for places to start new colonies.

Our most common termites live in nests in the ground. The ones in the picture are all workers except for two large-jawed soldiers.

Above: In spring, king and queen termites with wings swarm
out of the nest. They pair off and start new colonies.
Below: Soon after pairing off, the queen sheds her wings.
In time, her abdomen gets very large because it is full
of eggs.

CHAPTER 4

INSECTS THAT SING

Many insects make sounds. Bees, flies, and mosquitoes make humming sounds when they fly. Scientists believe that some of these sounds may be a sort of language used by the insects to attract mates. The buzzing of other insects such as bees warns us that they are angry and may sting us if we bother them.

The most familiar insect sounds are the songs of katydids, crickets, and cicadas. These insects perch in trees and often sing for long periods. Only the males sing. A katydid's tune may not seem very pretty to our ears, but to the female insect it is probably very pleasing. He sings to attract her. It is really a love song.

Crickets, katydids, and some grasshoppers make their chirping sounds by rubbing one part of their bodies against another. This kind of sound-making is called *stridulation*. It is like the bow crossing the strings of a violin or cello.

Many insects saw out their tunes at sunset, or after dark. If you sit out of doors at those times you may hear them, especially if you sit near trees.

A black field cricket

All singing insects sing faster in warm weather than they do in cool weather.

CRICKETS

The best-known insect songsters are probably black field crickets. They are about an inch long and are found almost everywhere. They sound as if they were saying, "Cree-kit, cree-kit." This of course is why they are called crickets. Black crickets do not live in trees. You can find them in clumps of grass or under old boards on the ground. Often they enter houses and hide behind furniture. They like warm places.

When a male cricket is in the mood to sing, he raises his wings over his back and saws them back and forth very rapidly. Usually this is done so fast that our eyes cannot see the movements of the wings.

A snowy tree cricket

Another songster is the snowy tree cricket. These crickets are also about an inch long, but are green. They live among the leaves of trees and bushes. Their songs sound like "churr-churr-churr."

KATYDIDS

Probably the songs of katydids are the loudest of all. There are several different kinds of katydids and each one has its own song. These insects are bright green, so they are not easy to see in the trees. Most of them are about two inches long. Their ears are on their front legs.

One kind of katydid sounds as if it were saying, "Katy-did-katy-didn't-she-did." To some people their calls sound like, "Katy-did, katy-did, katy-did." Other kinds of katydids have different calls. The angular-winged katydid says, "Click-click-click."

Angular-winged katydid

Above: When the angular-winged katydid sings, it raises
its front wings and moves them rapidly back and forth.
Below: The "true" katydid lives high in trees.

The bush katydid says, "Zeet-zeet-zeet."

Like the crickets, katydids make their sounds by raising their front wings and sawing them back and forth. Near the base of one wing there is a row of teeth. On the other wing there is a blade-like scraper. When the scraper is moved rapidly back and forth across the teeth, a loud sound is made. This is the song of the katydid.

CICADAS

The common cicada is found almost everywhere in the United States and in many other countries. These insects are often called "locusts," but they are not really locusts. Locusts are a kind of grasshopper.

Cicadas are about two inches long and have four, cellophane-like wings. When the insects are resting, the

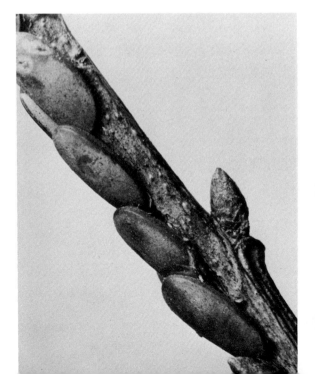

Katydids lay their disc-shaped eggs on twigs. The eggs hatch in the spring.

39

A cicada

wings are folded roof-like over their backs. Young
cicadas live in the ground where they suck out the juices
of tree roots. Some young cicadas stay underground
for as long as seventeen years. When full grown these
young cicadas come out of the ground and change into
adults with wings. The adults do not eat and so do not
live very long. They perch in trees and the males sing
loudly all during the daylight hours. They never sing at
night as the crickets and katydids do.

Cicadas are the drummers of the insect world. There is
a pair of drums on the underside of each male. Small
muscles in the cicada's body make these drums *vibrate,*
or snap in and out. Cicadas can often be heard for
several hundred feet. Few other insects have such loud calls.

CHAPTER 5

INSECTS OF WOODS AND FIELDS

Summer is the time to see insects in fields and woods.
Many kinds stay in the egg stage during the winter.
Others hide under the bark of trees. Still others stay hidden
in the ground during the cold months. In the spring,
insects of many kinds come out from eggs or from the
places where they have spent the winter.

GRASSHOPPERS

Eggs of short-horned grasshoppers, laid in the ground
in the fall, begin to hatch in spring. The young 'hoppers
come up out of the ground and eat grass or other plants.
Hungry birds find and eat many of them. The rest grow
up and become adults with wings. They fly away across
the field if we disturb them. These insects are known
as short-horned grasshoppers because they have short
antennae, or feelers.

In open fields you may see other grasshoppers. These
are pretty insects, colored bright green or greenish-
brown. Their antennae are very long, often longer than
their bodies. That is why they are called long-horned

Above: The short-horned grasshopper has large hind legs
for jumping, and short antennae or "feelers."
Below: The long-horned grasshopper is usually green
and has very long antennae.

grasshoppers. There are many different kinds. Some sing. You can often hear them sawing out their tunes on summer days. Some long-horned grasshoppers lay their eggs in the ground. Others lay them in twigs or attach them to leaves or stems. Grasshoppers often harm crops.

PRAYING MANTISES

The praying mantises spend the winter as eggs. Often, in winter, you can see their eggs on the stems of plants or on twigs. In spring the eggs hatch. At once the tiny mantises capture and eat small insects, such as plant lice. As the mantises grow larger, they eat larger game. By

The praying mantis lays its eggs in clusters on twigs. The eggs will hatch in spring.

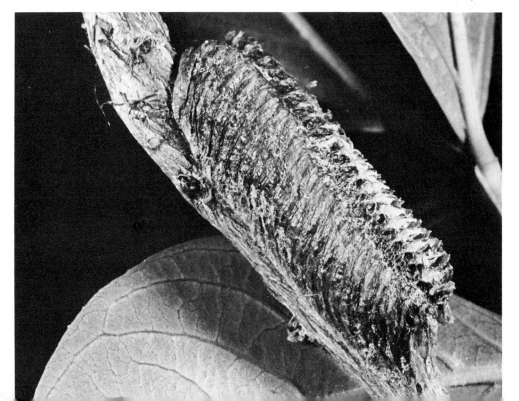

The praying mantis eats insects that it captures with its spiny front legs.

late summer they are full grown and have wings. A mantis is a most interesting insect to watch. It is always hungry. It eats grasshoppers, butterflies, or any other insect it can capture. It spends most of its time perching quietly in leaves, often near flowers that flying insects visit. The mantis is green and not easy to see. When an insect comes close enough, the spiny forelegs of the mantis flash out, and the unfortunate insect is captured. Then it is slowly eaten.

There are several kinds of praying mantises, but they all capture insects with their spiny forelegs. They hold these forelegs in front of their bodies as if they were praying. This is why they are called praying mantises. But the mantis is not praying, as any insect that comes too near may find out.

44

Not many insects can move their heads freely, but mantises can. A mantis will usually watch anything moving nearby. If you are careful not to crush it, you can pick one up, keep it in a small cage, and give it other insects to eat.

WALKINGSTICKS

First cousins to the mantises are the walkingstick insects. These slender insects eat only plants. They crawl slowly among the leaves. Because they look like twigs, they are not easy to see. When full grown the female walkingstick drops her eggs to the ground. They stay there, hidden in dead leaves, until the next spring when they hatch.

A walkingstick insect on a tree.

CRICKETS

On almost every walk through the fields in summer you may see black field crickets. Sometimes they will hop away from you across open places. Mostly they hide in grass near the ground. Often they are found under boards or stones. Like grasshoppers, their back legs are large and well fitted for jumping. They eat plants and lay their eggs in the ground. These crickets often enter houses and hide behind the furniture. Sometimes, especially at night, their chirping calls can be heard.

PLANT OR TREE GALLS

While walking in woodlands never be in a hurry. There are almost always many things to be seen if you take the time to look for them, and have sharp eyes. You may see large growths that look like apples attached to the leaves and twigs of trees, especially oaks. These are called apple galls. If you cut one open, you will find a small grub inside. These grubs are the young of small wasps that lay their eggs on the leaf or twig. When the eggs hatch into grubs, the tree grows the galls around them. Inside the galls the grubs are surrounded by food and are safe from most enemies.

Plant galls are found on many other plants, such as goldenrod. Goldenrod galls are found wherever these plants grow. They are knot-like swellings on the stems. A plump grub lives in each of the swellings. These grubs are the young stage of a pretty fly.

46

Above: An oak-tree apple
gall. They are green with dark
spots and about an inch
across.
Below: Goldenrod galls.

Look for galls of other kinds. Some have very strange shapes and are often very pretty. Cone-shaped galls are often seen on witch-hazel leaves. They are the homes of plant lice. Wool-sower galls, found on oak twigs, look like balls of pink wool. They are the homes of tiny wasps. Spiny galls are often seen on the stems of rose and blackberry bushes. These galls are the size of marbles and are covered with many sharp spines.

Spring is the best time to look for galls.

CATERPILLARS

Caterpillars are the young of moths and butterflies. There are many different kinds and we usually find them feeding on the leaves of trees and plants. Some caterpillars are hairy or spiny, while the bodies of others are bare. Some kinds are very colorful. As a general rule, the spiny or hairy kinds will turn into moths.

One of the common caterpillars is the woolly bear. These caterpillars are brown in the middle and black at each end. When full grown they are about an inch and a half long. You often see them crawling across highways, especially in autumn. In the spring they change into Isabella tiger moths.

Some spiny caterpillars are quite poisonous. Leave them alone!

MOTHS

Moths are common everywhere. They often come to lights at night, but sometimes we see them clinging

This is a saddleback caterpillar. It is greenish in color and has on its back a green spot centered with brown. Its sharp spines are very poisonous.

to leaves or tree trunks during the day. Usually, when at rest, moths fold their wings roof-like over their backs. Their antennae, or feelers, are either thread-like or feather-like. The antennae of butterflies are different. They have little clubs at their tips. Some moths, such as luna and cecropia moths, are large and very beautiful. Other moths are small and either gray or brown.

A luna moth. They are often seen in the woods. They are light green with purple edges on their wings.

BUTTERFLIES

Butterflies of a few kinds may be found in woods, especially where there are open places. You will see most of them in open fields or flower gardens where there are many flowers. They light on the flowers to sip their sweet nectar.

The large swallowtails are probably the best known. They perch lightly on flowers, slowly fanning their wings back and forth as they drink the nectar. There are several different kinds. One of the largest is the tiger swallowtail. Its wings are bright yellow with black markings. Its caterpillars have two eye spots near the

Tiger swallowtail butterfly. They are about 4 inches across.

Dog's-head butterfly. It is about 1½ inches across.

front end of the body. They eat the leaves of birch, poplar, and other trees.

Also common in fields are the little sulphur butterflies. Their caterpillars eat clover and other plants. We often see them flitting about, their yellow wings flashing in the sun. Usually their wings are marked with black.

The dog's-head is one of the most interesting sulphur butterflies. On each front wing there is a perfect "picture" of a dog's head with an eye. The dog's head is yellow, surrounded by black. This makes it one of the easiest butterflies to identify.

Cloudless sulphur butterflies have lemon-yellow wings and are nearly 2 inches across.

During late summer you will see large sulphur butterflies. These have no dark markings on their wings. That's why they are called cloudless sulphur butterflies. They are common in the eastern United States. The strange thing is that almost every one you see in autumn will be flying toward the south or southeast. For this reason people often call them "the butterflies that fly south." They flit across fields, through forests, or over houses, always going in the same direction. In spring they are sometimes seen flying north.

The monarch is one of the best-known butterflies. It is about four inches across. Its rust-red wings have black markings. It flies south in autumn as many birds do. Its caterpillars eat milkweeds.

The well-known monarch butterfly in flight.

CHAPTER 6

INSECTS OF PONDS AND STREAMS

Some of our most unusual insects live on or in the water.
Most may be found wherever there are pools, lakes,
or rivers.

DRAGONFLIES

Dragonflies dart gracefully over the water. Their
cellophane-like wings flash in the summer sun. Now and
then they alight on sticks. Then they are off again,
circling above the water.

Some dragonflies are nearly five inches across and are
high flyers. Others are much smaller and don't fly
more than a foot above the water. They all have very good
eyesight.

The skimmers are among the largest of all dragonflies.
One kind is the widow. It is about four inches across and
the inside of each wing is black. Another is the white-tail.
Its tail is white and there is a black band across the
center of each wing.

Dragonflies eat small gnats and mosquitoes which they

Above: Dragonflies light on twigs and plants near water. They rest with outspread wings. This is a widow dragonfly. It gets its name from the black marking at the base of its wings. Below: Dragonflies have very large eyes and can see in all directions. This helps them to capture the insects they eat and to escape enemies.

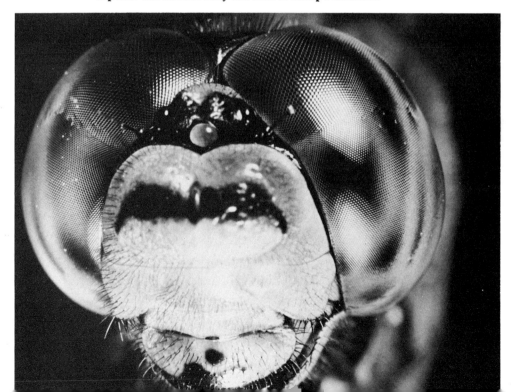

capture in the air. They are often known as the hawks
of the insect world.

Young dragonflies live in the water and have interesting
habits. Their lower lips have jaws that can be pushed
out in front of their heads to catch small water insects.
They can even catch and eat small fish. These young
dragonflies are called *nymphs* and they live in the water
for a year or two. Then they crawl up out of the water
and their skins split open. Out crawl the winged dragonflies.
At first their wings are crumpled up, but they slowly
open out. Then the adult dragonflies are ready for flight.

Dragonfly young, or nymphs, live in ponds and streams.

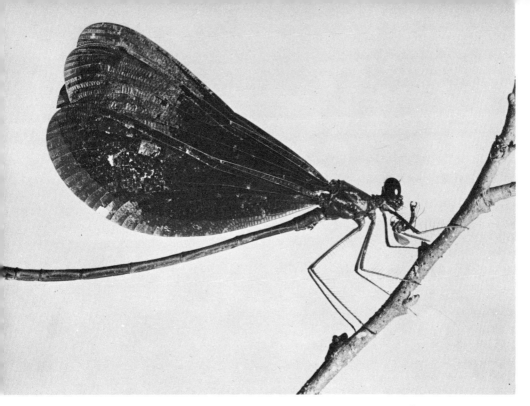

Damselflies light on twigs and fold their wings over their backs. This black-winged damselfly is eating a gnat.

DAMSELFLIES

The smaller damselflies are closely related to the dragonflies. You can tell a damselfly from a dragonfly by the way it holds its wings when it perches on a twig. Damselflies fold their wings over their backs, and dragonflies spread their wings out flat. Some kinds of damselflies are very pretty. The ruby-spot has a bright red spot at the base of each wing. Another is the black-winged damselfly. They are usually seen along woodland streams. The life histories of damselflies are like those of dragonflies.

WATER-STRIDERS

Along the edges of ponds or streams we often see long-legged insects running about over the surface of the water. These are water-striders. If you look closely you will see that their feet make tiny dimples on the water as they run about. They are able to do this because their feet are covered with oil and they do not sink into the water. They capture and eat small insects.

UNDERWATER INSECTS

So far we have talked about insects that live mostly above the surface of the water. There are many other kinds that live on the bottoms of streams or ponds, or among water plants that grow there. You can't see them unless the water is clear.

Water-striders are often called "water skaters."

The water boatman lives under the surface of the water.

If you wish, you can scoop water insects up with a net or a dipper and place them in a glass jar or an aquarium. Then you can watch them and study their habits.

One common water insect is the water boatman. These insects are about an inch long. They have long legs which they use like oars to paddle themselves through the water. They eat small water insects.

The giant water-bugs are much larger than the water

This giant water-bug is catching a minnow.

boatmen. They are often three inches long. Their
bodies are flattened. They have very sharp beaks and can
bite your fingers if you are not careful. They, too, have
oar-like legs for swimming. Giant water-bugs eat water
insects that they capture with their long front legs.
They also capture tadpoles and minnows and have been
known to kill small water snakes.

Water scorpions are unusual pond insects. You will
often find these hiding among water plants. Their
bodies are long and slender. Long breathing tubes are
attached to their tails. These tubes are pushed up to
the water's surface to get air. Their forelegs are shaped

like those of the praying mantis and are used in the same way to capture insects.

If you look carefully in clear pools or mountain streams you may see caddis insects. These are very interesting because they build small tubes or cases to live in. These cases protect them from enemies.

Caddis insects look something like caterpillars and are the young of caddis-flies. They lay their eggs in the water. The caddis insects that hatch from the eggs build their tube cases out of different kinds of materials. Some use small pebbles, others use pieces of bark, while others

The water scorpion lives among water plants.

This caddis insect has built its case of pebbles. When full grown it will change into a winged caddis fly and leave the water.

cement small twigs together crosswise so that their cases look like little log cabins. When a caddis insect wishes to move about, it pushes its head and legs out of its case and drags the case along behind itself. The habits of caddis insects may be studied in an aquarium. Perhaps you may even see them building their cases.

Water beetles live under the surface. Like water boatmen, they have oar-like legs for swimming.

INDEX

(Numbers in italics indicate pictures)